IRON

A TRUE BOOK®

by
Salvatore Tocci

Children's Press®
A Division of Scholastic Inc.

New York Toronto London Auckland Sydney
Mexico City New Delhi Hong Kong
Danbury, Connecticut

Reading Consultant
Julia McKenzie Munemo, EdM
New York, New York

Content Consultant
John A. Benner
Austin, Texas

The photo on the cover shows products made of iron. The photo on the title page shows Inuit tools made of iron.

The author and the publisher are not responsible for injuries or accidents that occur during or from any experiments. Experiments should be conducted in the presence of or with the help of an adult. Any instructions of the experiments that require the use of sharp, hot, or other unsafe items should be conducted by or with the help of an adult.

These people are walking across an iron bridge.

Library of Congress Cataloging-in-Publication Data

Tocci, Salvatore.
Iron / by Salvatore Tocci.
    p. cm. — (A true book)
    Includes bibliographical references and index.
    ISBN 0-516-23695-4 (lib. bdg.)   0-516-25571-1 (pbk.)
    1. Iron—Juvenile literature. I. Title. II. Series.
QD181.F4T63 2005
546'.621—dc22   2004013146

Contents

Although there are billions of stars, you can see only about three thousand of them on a clear night.

How Is a Star Born?

Have you ever tried to count the stars shining in the sky on a moonless night? If you have, you may have given up because you thought there were simply too many to count. Did you ever wonder where all these stars came from?

A star begins as a cool cloud made of gases and dust. A force pulls the gases and dust inward, causing the cloud to collapse. The gases get hotter and hotter as the cloud collapses, giving off light. Most of the gas is hydrogen, which is an element. An **element** is the building block of matter. **Matter** is the stuff or material that makes up everything in the universe, including you, this book, and stars.

The center of the collapsing cloud may get hot enough for hydrogen particles to fuse, or join together. This joining produces a heavier element called helium. At this point, the cloud of hydrogen, helium, and dust has become a star. The closest star to Earth, our Sun, is making helium from hydrogen right now.

When the supply of hydrogen starts to run out, some stars begin to fuse helium atoms. This process makes even heavier elements, such as carbon and oxygen. The process stops when these stars make the heaviest element they can. This element is iron.

When Was the Iron Age?

In addition to a name, every element has a symbol that consists of one, two, or three letters. The symbol for iron is Fe. This symbol comes from *ferrum*, the Latin word for iron. The ancient Romans used iron mainly to make tools and weapons. However, the use of iron goes back much farther in time. More than five thousand years ago, the ancient Egyptians used iron to make small objects, such as beads, to wear. The Egyptians got the iron from **meteorites**. A meteorite is a solid object that lands on Earth after traveling through space. Not very many meteorites land on Earth. As a result, the supply of iron was very limited.

A meteorite is what lands on Earth after a meteor breaks apart as it passes through Earth's atmosphere.

These objects are Iron Age axes, which were made over three thousand years ago.

About 3,500 years ago, people discovered that they could get iron from within Earth. As a result, they were able to use iron to build many more objects, including the utensils they used for cooking. This discovery marked the start of the Iron Age, which lasted for almost one thousand years.

Iron is an element commonly found in Earth's crust,

or outermost layer. Iron, however, is not found as a pure element in the crust. It exists as part of a **compound**, which is a substance made of two or more combined elements. There are millions of different compounds. However, there are just a few more than one hundred different elements, including iron.

How can so many different compounds be made up of so

few elements? Think about the English language. Just twenty-six letters can be arranged to make up all the words in the English language. Likewise, the one hundred or so different elements can be arranged to make up all the different compounds that exist.

Many compounds that contain iron are called **ores**. During the Iron Age, separating the iron from the other

Hematite

Magnetite

These are just a few ores that contain iron.

Limonite

elements in an ore was a difficult job. The ore had to be heated to a very high temperature over charcoal fires built in large clay ovens. The ore was then cooled and hammered. This process separated the iron from the other elements in the ore.

What Is Iron Used For?

Soon after the Iron Age started, the Chinese developed a method for making cooking utensils from cast iron. These utensils were made by pouring the hot melted iron extracted from ores into a mold, or cast. After the iron had cooled,

This stove is made of cast iron.

the object was removed
from the cast and was ready
to use.

This railing is made of wrought iron.

The next step in the use of iron involved making objects from wrought iron. Wrought iron is made by heating iron until it glows white. It is then hammered or pounded into various shapes. The ancient Romans used this process to make armor for their soldiers as well as door locks, hinges, and handles. Today, pieces of wrought iron are joined to make furniture, gates, and railings.

Iron can be used to make these objects because it is **malleable**. This means iron can be pounded into various shapes without breaking. This property places iron in a group of elements known as metals. One feature that all metals share is their ability to conduct electricity. Iron is a good **conductor** of electricity.

Iron, like most metals, is reactive. This means iron

Because iron is malleable, a blacksmith can hammer it into different shapes when it is hot.

Rust is a compound made of two elements, iron and oxygen.

reacts, or combines, very easily with other elements to form compounds. One element that iron reacts with very easily is oxygen, which is present in air and water. The compound that forms when iron and oxygen combine is commonly called rust. Iron must be protected so that it does not react with oxygen to form rust.

Protecting Iron

Find out how you can protect iron from rust. Clean and dry three iron nails. Cover one lightly with any type of oil. Cover another with any type of paint. Leave one untouched. Clean and dry one galvanized nail. A galvanized nail is made by coating the iron with a thin layer of zinc, which is another element. Use a file to scratch off a small section of zinc so the iron is exposed.

Place the four nails, including the one that has been untouched, in a plastic lid. Dissolve 2 tablespoons (30 milliliters) of table salt in a glass of water. Sprinkle the nails with the salt water. Examine the nails every day for about a week. Keep the nails moist with the salt water. Which nails do not rust?

Although iron has many uses, it is not strong enough to support a huge weight, such as a building, bridge, or large ship. During the Iron Age, people discovered a way to make iron stronger. They heated iron to a very high temperature. They then added one or more other elements before allowing the liquid to cool. What they had made was steel.

The method used today to make steel was developed in the 1850s.

Steel is an example of an **alloy**. An alloy is made by mixing a metal, such as iron, with one or more other elements.

Carbon is the main element added to iron to make steel. The more carbon that is added, the stronger the steel is. For example, the steel used to make a pair of scissors contains nearly twenty times as much carbon as the steel used to make a paint or garbage can. However, the steel used to make a pair of scissors still contains less than 1.5 percent carbon.

Although it is stronger than iron, steel still rusts. Adding

These utensils are made of stainless steel.

other elements besides carbon creates a steel alloy that will not rust. This is called stainless steel. Stainless steel gets its name from the fact that it is resistant to rusting, or "stains less."

Besides being used to make objects and structures that we use every day, iron is also critical for keeping our bodies healthy. Iron is part of a substance in red blood cells called **hemoglobin**. Hemoglobin picks up oxygen in the lungs and carries it in the blood to every cell in the body. Cells use oxygen to produce energy.

Our bodies get the iron they need from foods. The

This spinach salad is rich in iron.

United States Recommended Dietary Allowance (USRDA) for anyone older than four years of age is 18 milligrams of iron per day. Grain products, such as breads, noodles, cereals, and rice, provide almost half of this amount. Other foods that are rich in iron include apricots, spinach, lima beans, pork, and clams.

A balanced diet usually provides all the iron our bodies need. If the body does not get enough iron, a condition called **anemia** may develop. Symptoms include a lack of energy, shortness of breath, dizziness, pale skin, and a rapid heartbeat.

Adding Extra Iron

Some foods, such as cereals, are enriched with iron. Paint a small magnet white. After it dries, place the magnet in a bowl. Add 1 cup of an iron-enriched cereal. Next, add 2 cups of warm water. Stir the cereal and water for at least fifteen minutes. Carefully remove the magnet from the bowl. The black specks are tiny pieces of iron that are attracted by the magnet.

Why Is Earth a Giant Magnet?

When iron is most of what is left in a star, the star explodes. The explosion is known as a **supernova**. A supernova releases a tremendous amount of energy into space. It releases enough energy to make elements that are heavier than iron and hurls them into space. They can then form such cosmic bodies as planets, including Earth.

When Earth was being formed, the iron it contained was heavy enough to sink toward the center of the planet. This iron is solid and makes up most of Earth's inner core. The inner core is surrounded by an outer core, which is

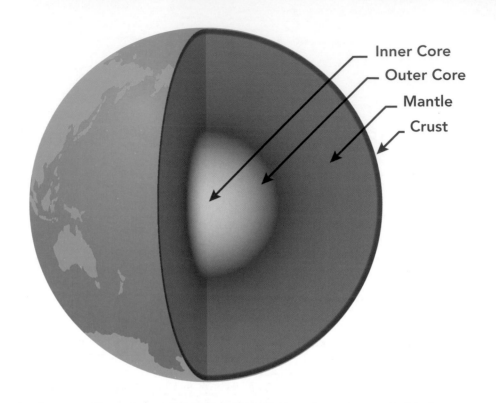

Inner Core
Outer Core
Mantle
Crust

Scientists think the temperature in Earth's inner core is at least 7,000 degrees Fahrenheit (3,870 degrees Celsius).

made mostly of liquid iron. Together, the inner and outer iron cores make Earth a giant magnet.

Like all magnets, Earth has a magnetic north pole and a magnetic south pole. A compass needle turns so that one end points to Earth's magnetic north pole, which is located in northern Canada. The other

Have you ever used a compass to find your way while hiking through the woods or sailing on a boat?

Antarctica is the site of Earth's magnetic south pole.

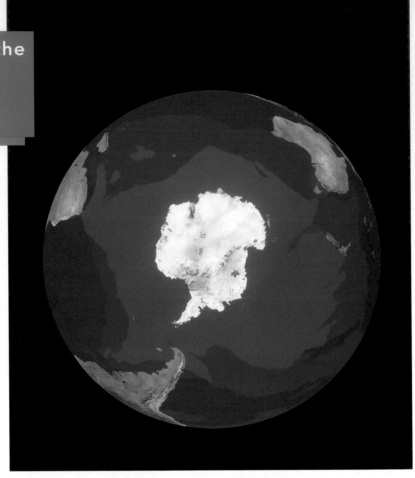

end of the compass needle points to Earth's magnetic south pole, which is located in Antarctica.

Neither magnetic pole remains in a fixed location. For example, the magnetic north pole moves about 45 yards (40 meters) northward each day. This movement is caused by the outer core of molten iron moving over the inner core of solid iron. The magnetic poles have wandered since Earth was first formed from the elements made by supernovas.

Fun Facts About Iron

- The Inuit once made their iron tools from a 30-ton meteorite known as Cape York that landed in Greenland.

- One of the world's largest dams is in Brazil. The amount of iron and steel used in this dam is enough to build 380 Eiffel Towers in Paris.

- An iron ore called chalcopyrite is known as "fool's gold" because it is often mistaken for real gold.

- The first battle between warships made of iron involved the *Monitor* and the *Merrimac* and took place in 1862 during the American Civil War.

- When the iron in hemoglobin combines with oxygen, the blood has a red color. When hemoglobin lacks oxygen, the blood has a purplish color.

- Because of the way iron acts in Earth's cores, the magnetic poles have reversed themselves several times since our planet was formed. About 800,000 years ago, the magnetic south pole was the magnetic north pole, and vice versa.

- Recycling the steel in just one car saves 2,500 pounds (1,130 kilograms) of iron ore.

To Find Out More

If you would like to find out more about iron, check out these additional resources.

 **Books**

Blashfield, Jean F. **Iron and the Trace Elements.** Raintree/Steck Vaughn, 2002.

Kassinger, Ruth. **Iron and Steel.** Twenty-First Century Books, 2003.

Sparrow, Giles. **Iron.** Benchmark Books, 1999.

Organizations and Online Sites

Why Is Mars Red?
http://www.athena.cornell.edu/kids/tommy_tt_issue2.html

Both Mars and the Moon contain iron. Learn why iron makes Mars look red while it causes the Moon to have dark spots. You can also find out more about the tiny particles called atoms that make up iron.

Blacksmithing Activities for Kids
http://www.earlyamericanmuseum.org/blacksmith_kids/blacksmithmenu.htm

Learn how people known as blacksmiths worked with iron. You can also hear what a blacksmith shop sounds like.

We Are All Star Stuff
http://stp.gsfc.nasa.gov/whats_hot/kids/all_star_stuff.htm

This site provides more information about supernovas. For example, learn what actually happens to the iron in a star and how this element becomes part of our bodies.

Roscoe's Recycle Room
http://www.recycle-steel.org/index2.html

Click on the kids site where you can read more fun facts about iron and steel. You can also join the club and enjoy fun games, recycling facts, and educational activities.

Surviving the Iron Age
http://www.historytelevision.ca/archives/survivingironage

Read how people survived during the Iron Age. Seventeen people describe their experiences with living as their ancestors did more than two thousand years ago.

Important Words

alloy substance made by mixing a metal with one or more other elements

anemia illness caused by lack of iron

compound substance formed when two or more elements are joined

conductor substance through which electricity or heat passes

element building block of matter

hemoglobin substance in red blood cells that transports oxygen

malleable capable of being hammered into different shapes without breaking

matter stuff or material that makes up everything in the universe

meteorite part of a meteor that reaches Earth

ore material found in nature from which a metal, such as iron, can be extracted

supernova massive explosion of a star that releases a huge amount of energy

Index

Meet the Author

Salvatore Tocci is a science writer who lives in East Hampton, New York, with his wife Patti. He was a high school biology and chemistry teacher for almost thirty years. His books include a high school chemistry textbook and an elementary school series that encourages students to perform experiments to learn about science. All the railings on his sailboat are made of stainless steel to protect against rust caused by exposure to salt water.

Photographs © 2005: Corbis Images: 12 (Archivo Iconografico, S.A.), 33 (Conde Nast Archive), 39 (Mark Cooper), 20 (Richard Cummins), 1 (Peter Harholdt), 23 (Paul A. Souders), 40 (Tom Van Sant); Envision/Steven Mark Needham: 31; Index Stock Imagery/Aneal Vohra: 2; Photo Researchers, NY: 19 (Jeffrey Greenberg), 29 (David Guyon/SPL), 11 (Jerry Lodriguss), 4 (Jerry Schad); Visuals Unlimited: 16 center (Carolina Biological), 16 bottom (Albert Copley), 24 (Jeff Daly), cover (Wally Eberhart), 16 top (Ken Lucas).

Illustration on page 38 by Bernard Adnet.